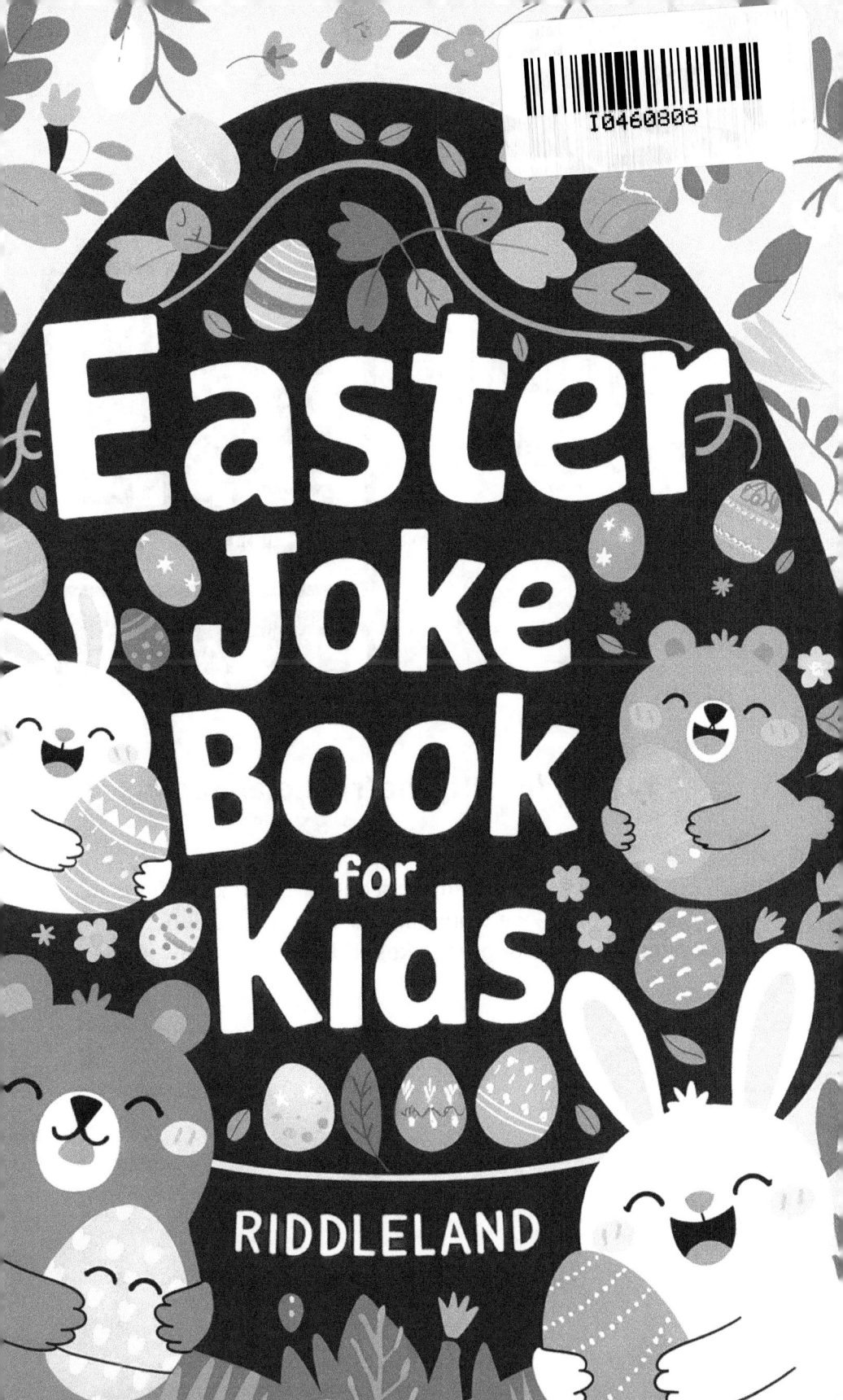

Easter Joke Book for Kids

RIDDLELAND

BONUS BOOK

FUN RIDDLES
AND
silly jokes
—— FOR ——
KIDS AND FAMILY

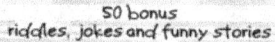

50 bonus
riddles, jokes and funny stories

RIDDLELAND

SCAN ME

https://pixelfy.me/riddlelandbonus

Thank you for buying this book. As a token of our appreciation, we would like to offer a special bonus-a collection of 50 original jokes, riddles, and funny stories.

INTRODUCTION

What is your favorite part about Easter? Dying eggs? Making baskets? Hunting what the Easter Bunny left for you? Donning new clothes? Attending worship? Having a family feast? Eating a chocolate rabbit? Something else?

No matter how you and your family celebrate Easter, the chances are that somebody is going to crack a good Easter-related joke. That person can be you.

Jokes liven up an event; jokes make an event memorable. In fact, some jokes are the highlight of the day, and family members share them year after year after that.

In this book, you will find 300+ jokes. They are not only good jokes; they are jokes with an Easter theme. The jokes in this book are original in the sense that they were not copied from other joke books, and they have been framed in a unique way, but the punchlines are very common in society. By memorizing your favorites, you'll be ready to pop off with a joke whenever the opportunity arises. Inside this book, you'll find question-and-answer jokes, puns, and knock-knock jokes, all with Easter themes, and a special section on eggs-amining your vocabulary.

You'll want to read this book cover to cover; you don't want to miss a thing. But, if you are in a hurry, the question-and-answer/punny jokes are categorized for your convenience, so you can go immediately to the subject matter that interests you at the moment. The book is broken into six chapters, or expos – question-and-answer jokes/ punny jokes, question-and-answer jokes/punny jokes, and knock-knock jokes, and knock-knock jokes. Now, as the Easter Bunny would say, "Let's hop to it and start reading."

TABLE OF CONTENTS

pg 3 Introduction

pg 6 Chapter 1:
Chickens, Hens and Roosters

pg 23 Chapter 2:
The Easter Bunny and his Bunny
Friends

pg 54 Chapter 3:
Chocolate Bunnies, Easter Lilies and
Easter Eggs

pg 69 Chapter 4:
Hot-Cross Buns and Jelly Beans

pg 76 Chapter 5:
Easter Baskets, Lent & Plastic Grass

pg 83 Chapter 6:
Easter Knock-Knock Jokes

CHAPTER 1
Chickens, Hens and Roosters

Question-and-Answer Jokes are probably the most common jokes kids tell. The joketeller asks a simple question, but the response that is expected in return is far from the serious response one would expect. In many cases, the response has a double meaning. What makes these punny ones funny is that one is not quite sure what the person meant to say. For instance, in the first joke, "cheep" can be the sound chickens make, but it sounds just like "cheap," meaning at low cost.

Meanwhile, in the second joke, "fowl" can mean birds, but it sounds just like "foul," which means vulgar and unacceptable. Words that sound the same but are spelled differently are called homophones. As you might suspect, one of the two meanings is often missed by the casual listener.

I asked a chicken what the price of eggs are? Do you know what he replied?

"Cheep! Cheep!"

Why should you avoid words like "geese," "chicken," "turkey," and "hen" around my mom?

She doesn't like to hear fowl words.

Which animal gives birth to psychics?

The chicken; it lays medium eggs.

Why was the hen worried when the Easter Bunny walked in front of her?

She was a hare behind where she wanted to be.

How is a henhouse like an onion?

It has many layers inside it.

Which direction does the Easter Hen move to lay her eggs?

Cluck-wise.

What type of movie do egg-laying hens enjoy?

A good chick flick.

What does the chicken do when she needs to do something she doesn't know how to do?

She wings it.

Who is the chicken's favorite classical composer?

"Bach! Bach! Bach!"

Why did the chicken study before trying to lay an Easter egg?

She wanted Grade A eggs.

Why couldn't the Easter Chicken locate her eggs?

She mislaid them.

What happened when the chickens got bored with laying eggs?

They wanted to fly the coop.

What does the chicken call his backpack?

"A bok-bok."

Why aren't most chickens creative?

They don't think outside the bawks.

What kind of products do chickens ask for by name?

Cheap.

What was the chicken glad to get out of the henhouse?

It was feeling cooped up.

How do hens dip their eggs in dye?

In one fowl swoop.

What did the hen say to the bully rooster?

"Peck on someone your own size."

What kind of outing does the Easter chicken enjoy?

A peck-nic.

Why are chicken coops such complex places?

They have many layers.

Why do chickens sit on eggs?

They can't find chairs.

Which animal can pilot farm buildings?

The chicken can fly the coop.

Why are actions more important to chickens than words?

Talk is cheap.

Which is the smelliest farm animal?

The chickens emit a fowl odor.

What did the chicken do when the farmer fed it and gave it a survey?

Gave him some feedback.

Why was the newborn chick so nervous?

She had shellshock.

Did you see the relay race?

The Easter Bunny took all the hens' eggs, and the hens had to re-lay more.

What did momma hen say to the shy hatchling?

"Come out of your shell."

What plant produces the most chickens?

The eggplant.

Do chickens always give up their eggs willingly?

No. Sometimes, you have to ruffle some feathers.

What do you call the hens that lay the Easter eggs?

Spring chickens.

What did the demon-possessed chicken offer the Easter Bunny?

Deviled eggs.

What did the chicken say on payday?

"Buck! Buck! Buck!"

What did the chicken check out at the library?

"Book! Book! Book! Book!"

Why were the hen's eggs triangular instead of oval?

She mislaid them.

What did the chicken say when the pitcher started to throw the baseball but didn't do it?"

"Balk! Balk! Balk! Balk!"

What did the chicken say when the farmer stood too close?

"Back! Back! Back! Back!"

How do chickens encourage each other?

They egg each other on.

How is an egg in armor like a match lighting dynamite?

One is "egg knight", and the other is ignite.

Why is the chicken willing to take the blame if the Easter eggs aren't perfect?

"Because the buck-buck-buck stops here."

How did the egg-laying chicken end its work shift?

She clucked out for the day.

How is an egg with a pimple like a door that leads outside?

One is an "egg zit", and the other is an "exit".

How is an egg starring in a play like a precise measurement?

One is "egg's act," and the other is "exact".

How is an egg in prison like a Microsoft computer program that does graphs?

One is "egg's cell," and the other is "Excel".

What did the pessimistic rooster crow at the start of the day?

"Cockadoodle-don't."

How is an egg wearing glasses like an enthusiastic cheerleader?

One is "egg sighted," and the other is "excited".

How is a terrible odor from an egg like a dinosaur?

One is "egg stink," and the other is "extinct".

How is a river with eggs floating in it like receiving a grade of A++?

One is "egg stream," and the other is "extreme."

How is an egg on a private island like a person who is banned from the tribe?

One is "egg's isle," and the other is "exile".

How is an egg that holds coins like kids swapping lunches?

One is an "egg's change," and the other is an "exchange".

How are eggs on a plate with a slice of ham like a test?

One is an "eggs-ham" combination, and the other is an "exam."

How are eggs an artist is drawing, like a picture of x-ray film that has seen light?

One is "eggs posed," and the other is "exposed."

How are two eggs resting on a bench like a fire escape?

One is an "eggs sit," and the other is an "exit".

How is the Easter hen able to lay all those eggs?

Hen-durance.

How are eggs on a plate with a leaf of spearmint like a science project?

One is "eggs-spearmint," and the other is "experiment".

What dessert do chickens like?

Coop cakes.

Why was the momma hen sad?

Her son wasn't being all she thought he was cracked up to be.

How much does a hen charge for each egg?

A bach.

What do chickens say to start a race?

"Last one there is a rotten egg."

How is an egg writing C-A-T on the grease board like a teacher asking the naughty boy to go to the principal's office?

One is "eggs spell," and the other is "expel".

Which muscles do chickens work on at the gym?

Their pecks.

What do you call a person who raises chickens?

A chicken tender.

How can the Easter Bunny afford to give away all those eggs?

His hens work for chicken feed.

Which social media platform do chickens use?

Face bawk.

Chapter 2
The Easter Bunny and his Bunny Friends

Would most people consider delivering eggs around the world in one night to be a good idea?

No, it's a hare-brained idea.

Where does the Easter Bunny prefer to store his sugar?

In suites.

How is the Easter Bunny like a brewery?

Both specialize in hops.

Where does the Easter Bunny stay while on vacation?

At a Hare B&B.

What is the Easter Bunny's philosophy of life?

"Don't worry; be hoppy."

Why do employees tread so carefully at the Easter Bunny's manufacturing plant?

They have to walk on eggshells.

What does the Easter Bunny do when something needs to be done in a hurry?

He hops to it.

What happened when the Easter Bunny found a library book about egg dying?

He checked it out.

Do you know what it means when the hens lay the eggs, and the rabbits inspect them?

Every bunny's a critic.

What kind of rabbit lives in your nose?

Nose hares.

What happened when the Easter Bunny got in trouble for littering?

He had a warren out for his arrest.

Was the result close when the rabbit and the tortoise had a rematch?

I'm not sure; I heard the race was won by a hare.

How does the Easter Bunny call a meeting to order when he needs to make a big announcement?

"Hare ye, hare ye . . ."

What do you call the Easter Bunny's cousin who administers laughing gas to dental patients?

The Ether Bunny.

In what school subject do rabbits excel?

Math: rabbits are known for multiplying.

Why did the cash-strapped Easter Bunny offer a dating site to his egg-providing friends?

He wanted to make hens meet.

What's the Easter Bunny's favorite part of a car?

The eggs-cellerator.

How does the Easter Bunny get all those eggs delivered in one night; is it luck or skill?

I vote luck; he's got four lucky rabbit's feet.

Is the Easter Bunny nervous?

He's a little jumpy.

Does the Easter Bunny pay the hens that lay the Easter eggs?

I heard the hens get chicken feed.

What did the Easter Bunny specialize in when he went to college?

Egg-onomics.

How did the Easter Bunny color his fur bright orange?

With hare spray.

Is the Easter Bunny's factory a busy place?

The employees are definitely hopping.

How does the Easter Bunny comb his fur?

With a hare brush.

Are the Easter Bunny's ears healthy?

They are a sound organ.

How is a row of Easter Bunny-shaped flower pots with seeds like a balding man?

One is a re-seeding hare line, and the other is a receding hairline.

Where does the Easter Rabbit like to practice skiing?

The bunny hill.

What did the Easter Bunny want on Valentine's Day?

Some bunny to love.

Where does the Easter Bunny live?

In his natural rabbitat.

What kind of dog does the Easter Bunny own?

A basket hound.

What did the frog call to the Easter Bunny to get his attention?

"Rabbit. Rabbit."

How is the Easter Rabbit wearing his hair this year?

In a bun.

How can you tell if a rabbit burrow is full of senior adults?

If you look closely, you'll notice some grey hares.

What's the Easter Bunny's favorite party game?

Musical Hares.

What does the Easter Bunny say at the start of a cheer?

"Hip hop . . . hooray!"

Why can't you believe what the Easter Bunny tells you?

Because it's hare-say.

What does the Easter Bunny become if he has to work outdoors in the high heat?

A hot cross bun.

Why couldn't all the rabbits fit in the cage?

The cage was a hare too small.

What did the Easter Rabbit make at his bakery?

Something bunny.

Why do people dress up as the Easter Bunny?

Because to hare is human.

What story interested the youthful Easter Bunny the most?

He was fascinated with his cotton tale.

If the Easter Bunny's tail fell off, where would he have to go?

To a re-tail store."

What kind of vehicle does the Easter Bunny drive at the beach?

A dune bunny.

How is the scope of a camera similar to two angry bunnies in a burrow?

Both have cross hares.

What happened when the boy was giving rabbits piggyback rides, and his dad said, "Boo."

All the hares on his back stood up.

What do the barber and the skinned-knee Easter Bunny have in common?

Hare cuts.

What kind of shoes does the Easter Bunny wear?

Nike Hare.

Do you know why the Easter Bunny sniffs outdoor air?

He nose.

Did you know that the Easter Bunny pays his workers with vegetables?

They all work for a celery.

What part of the Easter Bunny must care be used in describing?

Detail.

Did you hear about the bunny that could command his tail to stop wiggling?

It was a tail of whoa.

What is the Easter Bunny's favorite letter of the alphabet?

It's the 24th letter, eggs.

Is it scary having baby rabbits as pets?

It's hare-raising.

Why did the Easter Bunny take his family to the barber shop?

To get hares trimmed.

Is the Easter Bunny creative when decorating eggs?

By every sketch of the imagination.

Where does the Easter Bunny store his eggs in the Arctic?

In an egg-loo.

Why did the Easter Bunny turn the thermostat in his henhouse to over 212 degrees?

He wanted to see if the hens would lay hard-boiled eggs.

What does classical music have in common with what the Easter Bunny does with eggs when he visits homes?

Haydin.

Is getting your picture made with the Easter Bunny scary?

It's hare-riffic.

How does the Easter Bunny leave a building?

Through the eggs-it.

Why is an Easter Bunny a rare sight after Easter?

Its eggs stink (extinct).

What did the embarrassed Easter Bunny say when someone pointed out his messy bookcase?

I'm ashamed of my shelf.

What happened when the Easter Bunny lost his temper?

He was hopping mad.

Why did the Easter Bunny ask for a stripe to be placed on an egg?

He wanted to draw the line.

How is the Easter Bunny like a cowboy?

Both are quick on the draw.

Was the Easter Bunny okay with using food coloring as egg dye?

He found the colors to be palatable.

What kind of shoes does the Easter Bunny wear when entering homes?

Sneakers.

Why does the Easter Bunny's egg factory show his character?

Because you can see the Easter Bunny's true colors there.

The Easter Bunny delivers Easter eggs; which rabbit delivers jokes?

The Easter Punny.

What can the funny bunny always deliver?

Laughs.

When the Easter Bunny was in a band, what genre of music did he play?

Hip hop.

Why does the Easter Bunny keep hopping with his basket unless he accidentally drops an egg?

His motto is "Hop 'til you drop."

How much are the Easter Bunny's two front teeth worth?

They are buck teeth.

What is the Easter Bunny's favorite time of day?

Hoppy hour.

Why did the Easter Bunny win an award?

He really delivered!

Why is the Easter Bunny so calm?

He boils his eggs so he never has to scramble.

What does the Easter Bunny say to motivate his workers?

"Hop to it."

What did the Easter Bunny say when asked why his tale was stubby?

"It may not be much, but I'm attached to it."

What does the Easter Bunny step on to get his car to go fast?

The eggs-celerator.

What does the Easter Bunny call a test?

"An eggs-am."

What does the Easter Bunny do if he is not paying attention?

Egg-nore.

What does an Easter Bunny say when he doesn't know anything about a subject?

"I am egg-norant about that."

What does the EasterBunny say if you do a good job?

"Eggs-cellent."

What kind of work does the Easter Bunny praise?

Eggs-ceptional.

If the easter Bunny wants a change to a norm, what does he ask for?

An eggs-ception.

If somebody almost sees the Easter Bunny as he hides eggs, what does he do?

Eggs-cape.

What makes a loud booming sound, according to the Easter Bunny?

An eggs-plosion.

What does the Easter Bunny call a trade?

"An eggs-change?"

When he gets excited, with what punctuation does the Easter Bunny end his sentences?

An eggs-clamation mark."

What does the Easter Bunny do when he inspects the eggs closely?

He eggs-amines the eggs.

What does the Easter Bunny call the door leading outside?

"The eggs-it."

What does the Easter Bunny call someone who is really smart?

An eggs-pert.

What does the Easter Bunny call leftover eggs?

"Eggs-tras."

What does the Easter Bunny call going to a jog?

"Eggs-ercise."

What does the Easter Bunny say instead of, "I'm tired"?

"I'm eggs-hausted."

What does the Easter Bunny call a tall tale?

"An eggs-aggeration."

What is the Easter Bunny's favorite type of music?

Hare metal.

How did the Easter Bunny do on his overnight hike?

He was a hoppy camper.

Why was the girl upset when the Easter Bunny sipped her milk?

She didn't like seeing a hare in her milk.

What did the Easter Bunny do while he was employed at the beauty salon?

Dye jobs.

How did the Easter Bunny feel after finishing his world tour?

He had lots of eggs and pains.

What was the Easter Bunny having when his oldest son misbehaved?

A bad hare day.

How is letting the Easter Bunny step into line in front of you like going to the barber for a trim?

Both are hare cuts.

What did the Easter Bunny's right ear say to his left ear?

"Between us, something smells."

What did the Easter Bunny say about his long-term plans?

"I have lots of hops and dreams."

What does the Easter Bunny call people who search out new lands?

"Eggs-plorers."

How does the Easter Bunny feel as Easter gets close?

"Eggs-cited."

What does the Easter Bunny use to find his misplaced keys?

A hare-tag.

Why is the Easter Bunny worried that his workers are going to mutiny?

He heard the hens discussing a coup.

What happened when the Easter Bunny learned to speak "frog"?

He became a bunny ribbit.

What does the Easter Bunny use if his fur gets wet in the rain?

A hare dryer.

What was the Easter Bunny's favorite type of stories as a young bun?

Tales.

What did the Easter Bunny, pretending to be a pirate, tell his crew about the treasure's location?

"Eggs marks the spot."

What bunny is even dirtier than the egg-dying Easter Bunny?

The dust bunny.

How well would the Easter Bunny say that you did you do if you got all these questions?

"Eggs-tremely well."

Who's going to be egg hunting on Easter?

Any bunny who's any bunny.

What does the Easter Bunny call a sample?

"An eggs-ample."

Why does the Easter Bunny get along with everyone so well?

Because he's egg-greeable.

Why is the Easter Bunny so special?

Because there is no bunny like him.

What kind of stories does the Easter Bunny tell?

Stories with hoppy endings.

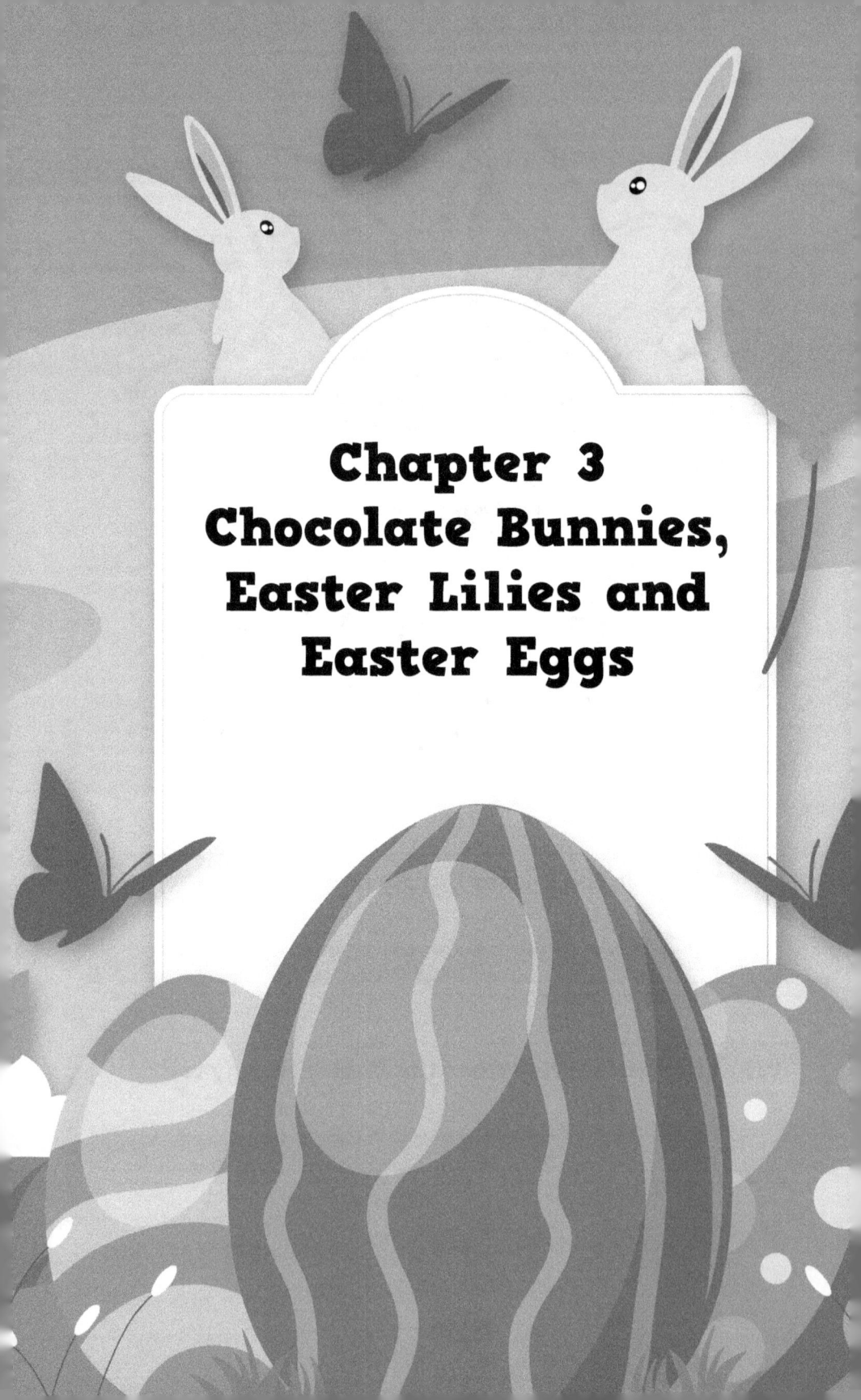

Chapter 3
Chocolate Bunnies, Easter Lilies and Easter Eggs

Chocolate Bunnies

Did you hear about the chocolate Easter Bunny that did crazy things?

People say he's a little nutty.

Why can you trust Easter chocolate to keep a secret, but you cannot trust Easter marshmallows to keep a secret?

Easter chocolate doesn't make a peep.

What did the chocolate bunny say when the bully tried to trick it?

"I ain't no sucker."

What did the chocolate bunny mutter when it was being wrapped in aluminum?

"Foiled again!"

What did the girl say as she handed her friend the tallest piece of chocolate bunny?

" 'ere's to you."

What happened when the boy offered his competitor some chocolate bunny?

They each had a peace of chocolate bunny.

Why did the chocolate rabbit open a bank account?

It was very rich.

Why did the girl put a chocolate bunny under her pillow?

She wanted sweet dreams.

Why do Easter chocolate rabbits taste so good?

They are choc-full of taste.

What did the chocolate rabbit say to the other chocolate rabbit who was sunbathing?

"You're a hot mess."

What do you call a stolen fudge rabbit?

Hot chocolate.

What did the romantic chocolate rabbit say to the girl?

"I'll melt in your hands."

What happened when the chocolate bunny got angry?

It had a meltdown.

Which chocolate rabbits are the most relaxed?

Those that are mallow.

What did the chocolate bunny say to the female chocolate bunny?

"You're sweet."

What did the chocolate bunny sigh as the girl bit into his ear?

"Ear today; gone tomorrow."

What did the boy chocolate rabbit say to the girl chocolate rabbit?

"You're making my heart melt."

Why was the chocolate rabbit so sad?

He felt hollow inside.

Why can't you trust a chocolate rabbit?

They fudge the truth.

Easter Lily

What did one young Easter Lily say to the other?

"Let's be buds."

How is the Easter Bunny building a new factory like a transplanted Easter Lily?

Both are putting down roots.

How is the letter A like an Easter lily?

A bee follows both of them.

Eggs

Why can't you tell an egg a secret?

It will crack under pressure.

Why do eggs hide?

They're a little chicken.

How did the egg call its friend?

On a shell-phone.

How did the teacher describe Junior's egg's behavior?

"He's a good egg."

How do you describe an egg the fox has stolen from the henhouse?

A poached egg.

Were the hen's eggs perfect?

They were to dye for.

What's an egg's favorite sport?

Sprinting: haven't you heard that eggs tend to run a lot?

How did the eggs get on the honor roll?

They were grade A.

How is a lawn on Easter morning like a video game?

Easter eggs are everywhere.

What happened when the boy fell face-first onto an unboiled Easter egg?

He had egg on his face.

In what metropolitan area do Easter eggs live?

New Yolk City.

What happens if you throw an Easter egg full-force at a cockroach?

The bug is eggs terminated.

What happens if more people make traditional Easter eggs this year than last year?

Making Easter eggs will still be a dying art.

Where will the Easter egg be hidden?

It will be in the last place you think to look. Once you find it, you won't look anywhere else.

Why is Easter egg hunting risky?

You put all your eggs in one basket.

Why does an Easter Egg Hunt have only two roles – find eggs or prepare eggs?

It's do or dye.

Why was the girl so embarrassed after swallowing food coloring?

She felt like she dyed a little inside.

What did the scared child say when his mother asked him to dip the egg in the food coloring?

"I'm too young to dye."

How did the detective know the girl had dyed the egg?

He caught her red-handed.

Why are there so few well-done eggs found on Easter morning?

Good eggs are hard to find.

Is it exciting watching egg dye dry?

It's as exciting as watching paint dry.

What did the Easter Bunny say when asked if he'd consider using non-boiled eggs?

"I might whisk it."

Was the egg mad?

It was boiling.

What did the dye say to the Easter egg?

"Relax; I've got you covered."

How do you prepare to paint eggs?

You brush up.

What did the paintbrush say to the egg?

"This may tickle a little."

Why was the striped egg so hard to find?

Because it wasn't spotted.

What did Mom say when she wanted Junior's help peeling Easter eggs?

"Let's get cracking."

How did the boy feel when he came across a hard chunk of something in his egg salad sandwich?

He was shell-shocked.

What happened when the eggs and bacon walked into a restaurant?

The hostess said, "I'm sorry, but we don't serve breakfast here."

What do you call two close friends who eat Easter eggs?

Taste buds.

Should you question what somebody is doing if you catch the person drawing on their Easter egg?

Yes, it is sketchy behavior.

Why is looking at beautiful Easter eggs so relaxing?

They are a master peace.

Which eggs are psychic?

The medium eggs.

What's the opposite of an Easter egg?

A Wester egg.

Are hard-boiled eggs the best Easter eggs?

They are hard to beat.

Why did the Easter Bunny lock the gym?

He didn't want any of his paint to run.

Is it easy to find uncooked Easter eggs?

They aren't hard.

Chapter 4
Hot-Cross Buns and Jelly Beans

Why did the hot cross bun flatter its friend?

It wanted to butter him up.

What was wrong with the blown-up photo of the hot cross bun?

The bun looked grainy.

How do you best describe a hot cross bun that has been raised properly?

Well, bread.

Why is the inventor of the biscuit honored?

He made a great roll model.

Which musical scale note is the hot-cross bun's favorite?

Dough.

Why did the boy place the dinner roll on his knee on Easter Day?

He wanted an Easter bun knee.

What should you say when you are about to eat a hot cross bun?

"Bun appetite."

What type of hotel is most likely to serve hot cross buns?

A bread-and-breakfast.

What did people yell as the hot cross bun waved goodbye from the cruise ship?

"Bun voyage."

Why does the Easter Bunny make hot-cross buns from scratch?

He kneads to relax.

What happened when the air conditioner broke at the Easter Bunny's paint factory?

There were a lot of hot cross buns.

How did the hot cross bun know he was ill?

He was feeling crumby.

What did the hot cross bun say to his girlfriend when he broke up with her?

"You deserve butter."

What did the hot cross bun say to his girlfriend on Valentine's Day?

"You're the only bun for me."

When the hot cross buns were in the oven, what did they say to motivate each other?

"Together, we rise."

What is an inventory of hot cross buns known as?

A roll call.

Why did the hot-cross-bun-eating boy say when asked if he was having fun at the dinner table?

"No, I'm having lots of bun."

Was the hot cross bun's baker rich?

He was rolling in the dough.

What did the hot cross bun become when the artist drew its picture?

A roll model.

Why did the boy place a stone beside his hot cross bun?

He wanted rock-and-roll.

What did Dad pun as he stood on a hot cross bun?

"Look, everybody. I'm on a roll."

Why do people relax eating hot cross buns?

It's fun to loaf.

Jellybeans

What kind of beans does the Easter Rabbit grow in his garden?

Jellybeans.

What mishap did the gossip have with her Easter basket?

She spilled the (jelly)beans.

Do jellybeans like Easter?

They have a soft spot.

What did the jellybean pack for its vacation?

A bean bag.

How do you describe a covering of jellybeans?

"Bean here. Bean there. Been everywhere."

How did the jellybean describe her Easter?

"It's bean wonderful."

Chapter 5
Easter Baskets, Lent
& Plastic Grass

Easter Baskets

Why does the Easter Bunny put cellophane over the basket?

He wanted to wrap up the project.

What did the egg say to the basket as it was placed inside the basket?

"I'm just along for the ride."

Was the Easter basket confident it could hold all the eggs?

It thought it could "handle" them.

Why was the basket so nervous?

It was a basket case.

Why was the Easter basket sad?

It felt empty inside.

What happened when the Easter basket got excited?

It got carried away.

What is a list that reads "basket, basket, basket, basket, basket, basket, basket, basket, basket, and basket"?

The Easter Bunny's bucket list.

What did the basket-maker say when his assistant told him that she was tired?

"Weave only just begun."

Jokes about Easter Jokes

Why aren't Easter jokes always original?

Some are Lent.

Why shouldn't you tell Easter jokes to eggs?

They'll crack up.

Why are jokes about the Easter Rabbit so popular?

They are very bunny.

Lent

How is someone who gives up driving and wears rollerblades for the Easter season like a machine that gathers fuzz from black pants?

Both are Lent rollers.

Why was the carpenter sad?

He gave up his vises for Lent.

Why can't you trust restaurant owners during Lent?

Most have very fishy menus, especially on Fridays.

What is the belly button's favorite part of the Easter season?

Lent.

What season is even more extreme than Easter?

Well, there is East, then there is Easter, so I guess the most extreme would be Easterest.

Plastic Grass

Why was the plastic Easter grass so self-confident?

It knew it wasn't going to get walked on.

Why don't more people have their lawns covered in plastic Easter grass?

Real grass will grow on you.

What did they call the contest between the real grass and the plastic grass?

A turf war.

Which has been around longer, real grass or plastic grass?

Real grass has roots; plastic grass does not.

Why did the artificial grass feel sad?

He kept comparing himself to greener pastures.

When the artificial grass wasn't damp, and he wanted it to have a touch of morning moisture, what did the Easter Bunny have to do?

Make dew.

How long has artificial grass existed?

For a lawn time.

What happened when the plastic grass was carried off?

It was lawn gone.

CHAPTER 6
Easter
Knock-Knock Jokes

Knock-Knock jokes may be eggs-actly what you need to make the mood festive. As the joke teller, you will read the first line. To help you keep your place, your lines are in bold. The other person will simply say, "Who's there?" and, having heard your answer, will seek clarification. You will then share the punny answer. Most people know the format of a knock-knock joke and will not need to read their lines.

Knock-Knock.
Who's there?
Ima Reilly.
Ima Reilly, who?
Ima Reilly big fan of Easter knock-knock jokes.

Knock-Knock.
Who's there?
Shelley Hans.
Shelley Hans, who?
Shelly Hans is what you will get if you peel Easter eggs.

Knock-Knock.
Who's there?
Hyde.
Hyde who?
Hyde the Easter eggs, and I'll try to find them.

Knock-Knock.
Who's there?
Phil D. Basket.
Phil D. Basket, who?
Phil D. Basket with candy and Easter eggs, please.

Knock-Knock.
Who's there?
Easter.
Easter who?
Easter (eased her) mind when I said Easter morning was going to be free of rain.

Knock-Knock.
Who's there?
Dye It.
Dye It, who?
Dye It is something I need to go on if I am going to lose weight.

Knock-Knock.
Who's there?
X.
X who?
X (eggs) are fun to find on Easter.

Knock-Knock.
Who's there?
Cottontail.
Cottontail who?
Cottontail what you were saying; can you say it again, please?

Knock-Knock.
Who's there?
Todd.
Todd who?
Todd some pretty good Easter jokes, haven't we?

Knock-Knock.
Who's there?
Pole Tree.
Pole Tree, who?
Pole Tree are needed if there are going to be eggs.

Knock-Knock.
Who's there?
Eggs.
Eggs who?
Eggs and pains are a part of running around looking for Easter eggs.

Knock-Knock.
Who's there?
Four Eggs.
Four Eggs, who?
Four Eggs-ample (for example), I think you are good at telling knock-knock jokes.

Knock-Knock.
Who's there?
Hare Say.
Hare Say who?
Hare Say is things you have heard but have not been proven as true; they are rumors.

Knock-Knock.
Who's there?
Gene Eric.
Gene Eric, who?
Gene Eric eggs are boring to me; I like mine dyed and covered in stickers.

Knock-Knock.
Who's there?
Eggs Sighted.
Eggs Sighted who?
Eggs Sighted to go on an Easter egg hunt.

Knock-Knock.
Who's there?
Hyden.
Hyden who?
Hyden my Easter candy, so you can't find it.

Knock-Knock.
Who's there?
Eggs Plain.
Eggs Plain, who?
Eggs Plain to me when the Easter Bunny is expected to come.

Knock-Knock.
Who's there?
Eggs Act.
Eggs Act who?
Eggs Act day of Easter varies from year to year.

Knock-Knock.
Who's there?
Bunny Fits.
Bunny Fits who?
Bunny Fits (benefits) of an indoor egg hunt include not getting wet if it rains and no bugs crawling on the eggs.

Knock-Knock.
Who's there?
Marty Graw.
Marty Graw who?
Marty Graw is the carnival before Lent.

Knock-Knock.
Who's there?
Eggs Sighted.
Eggs Sighted who?
Eggs Sighted about going on an Easter egg hunt.

Knock-Knock.
Who's there?
Diego.
Diego who?
Diego in the Easter basket.

Knock-Knock.
Who's there?
One Two.
One Two who?
One Two tell some more knock-knock Easter jokes.

Knock-Knock.
Who's there?
Hare.
Hare who?
Hare we go, telling more good jokes.

Knock-Knock.
Who's there?
Hare.
Hare who?
Hare-larious jokes we are telling.

Knock-Knock.
Who's there?
Hare.
Hare who?
Hare what I have to say – Happy Easter!

Knock-Knock.
Who's there?
Rabbit.
Rabbit who?
Rabbit up in there; other people need a turn, too.

Knock-Knock.
Who's there?
Holly Days.
Holly Days, who?
Holly Days like Easter make me giddy.

Knock-Knock.
Who's there?
Earl Lee.
Earl Lee, who?
Earl Lee risers get to see the Easter sun come up.

Knock-Knock.
Who's there?
Dye? No, sir.
Dye? No, sir, who?
Dye? No, sir, goes r-r-r-r-r-r-r-roar!

Knock-Knock.
Who's there?
Heidi.
Heidi who?
Heidi eggs really well so it takes me a while to find them.

Knock-Knock.
Who's there?
Eggs Aisle.
Eggs Aisle, who?
Eggs Aisle occurs when one is barred from one's native country.

BONUS BOOK

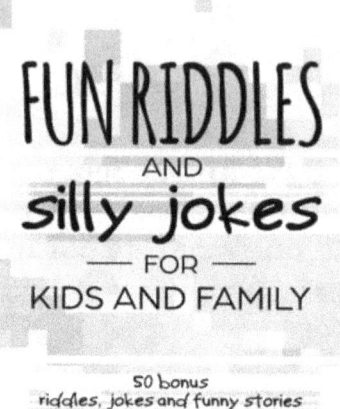

FUN RIDDLES
AND
silly jokes
— FOR —
KIDS AND FAMILY

50 bonus
riddles, jokes and funny stories

RIDDLELAND

SCAN ME

https://pixelfy.me/riddlelandbonus

Thank you for buying this book. As a token of our
appreciation, we would like to offer a special bonus-a
collection of 50 original jokes, riddles, and funny stories.

DID YOU ENJOY THE BOOK?

If you did, we are ecstatic. If not, please write your complaint to us and we will make sure to fix it.

If you're feeling generous, there is something important that you can help me with – tell other people that you enjoyed the book.

Ask a grown-up to write about it on Amazon. When they do, more people will find out about the book. It also lets Amazon know that we are making kids around the world laugh. Even a few words and ratings would go a long way.

If you have any ideas or jokes that you think are super funny, please let us know. We would love to hear from you. Our email address is -

riddleland@riddlelandforkids.com

ABOUT RIDDLELAND

Riddleland is a mum + dad run publishing company. We are passionate about creating fun and innovative books to help children develop their reading skills and fall in love with reading. If you have suggestions for us or want to work with us, shoot us an email at riddleland@riddlelandforkids.com

Our family's favorite quote:

"Creativity is an area in which younger people have a tremendous advantage since they have an endearing habit of always questioning past wisdom and authority."
~ Bill Hewlett

www.ingramcontent.com/pod-product-compliance
Lightning Source LLC
Chambersburg PA
CBHW061708120626
46550CB00003B/1142